D1078829

30 Days with Elijah

30 Days with Elijah

A devotional journey
with the prophet

Emily Owen

Authentic

20 19 18 17 16 15 14   7 6 5 4 3 2 1

First published in 2014 by Authentic Media Limited
52 Presley Way, Crownhill, Milton Keynes, MK8 0ES.
authenticmedia.co.uk

British Library Cataloguing in Publication Data
A catalogue record for this book is available from the British Library
ISBN: 978-1-86024-937-2   978-1-78078-256-0 (e-book)

Cover design by David McNeill revocreative.co.uk
Printed and bound by Bell & Bain Ltd, Glasgow.

Earnestly: with sincere & intense conviction

James 5:17 : Elijah prayed earnestly, prayed passionately & then took action

Nehemiah
Jerusalem

- Church born out of a prayer meeting
- Prepared to move - God uses us as part of the answer to our own prayers
- PLAY MY PART. - Speak God's heart onto friendships (not a waste)

Palace to Wilderness (Boot camp)

Peace, Preparation & Provision (Bear Grylls, Commanded to Hide Himself (boot camp)
↳desire to be known & not lonely
↳ Be still - solitude - spiritual discipline - slow down - Don't do do.

+ 3 years training → changed character - cares about heart. Phil 4:19
"Today God I need you"

Isolation + of amily · Easy to be spiritual at Mercy → challenge is living out the lessons in family environment.

Obedient in Ordinary *consistency in my character*
James

[I]f my [God's] people, who are called by my name, will humble themselves and pray and seek my face and turn from their wicked ways, then will I hear from heaven . . .

2 Chronicles 7:14

From: Tishbe in Gilead. (Gilead was an area with mountains, hills and forests and was good for grazing animals.)

The first thing we find out about Elijah in the Bible is his name.

Meanings of names were important in biblical times and everyone who met Elijah would know what his name meant – the Lord is my God.

Some people do still choose their children's name by meaning, but name meanings are not always as vital today as they were in biblical times.

Maybe you know what your name means, maybe you don't; but, either way, you can be an Elijah – you can show people you meet that the Lord is your God.

You can show it through how you live.

Through what you say.

Through how you spend your time.

Through what your priorities are.

Through how you react to difficult situations . . .

The Lord is your God – Be an Elijah!

Emily

Introduction

Elijah's diary will take you on a journey with the prophet Elijah.

You will share in the ups and downs of his walk with God as he strives to follow God's plan for his life.

Each day's reading ends with 'Be an Elijah'. This is a challenge, stemming from either the day's diary entry or its application, to keep in mind throughout the day and to be remembered when situations happen or people cross your path.

The 'my response' bit which follows is for you to use in any way you'd like. Maybe to record thoughts, feelings, actions or aims that have stemmed from the day's reading.

Please do read the biblical accounts, particularly in the books of 1 Kings and 2 Kings, from which I gathered the information for Elijah's diary. Remember that anything not found written in these accounts is conjecture.

I pray that Elijah's diary will inspire you, challenge you, encourage you and draw you closer to God.

So, just who was Elijah?

Name: Elijah, meaning 'the Lord is my God'.

Day 1

I'm Elijah and I've decided to keep a diary.

I had a strange day recently. In the morning, I went to King Ahab's palace. (He's the king of Israel.) I didn't go for a banquet or celebration, unfortunately – maybe next time?! I went because I had to tell him that there will be no rain in the land for the next few years. No rain until God decides to send some. It seems a strange message and I wasn't sure how the king would react – but God told me to say it, so I did.

After I'd told Ahab about the rain (or lack of), God's next instructions were for me to go and hide near the Jordan river. Wonder why I have to hide? Anyway, God told me to drink water from the brook there and to eat food that – wait for it – ravens will bring me?

Imagine you are Elijah.
You've gone from the presence of the king to hiding, camping out on your own, in a short space of time. Quite a change!
Maybe, as he sat on his own by the river, day after day, Elijah looked back to his time with the king with nostalgia.
Elijah had been quite important that day.

He'd been in the presence of the king, spoken to the king, delivered God's message to the king . . . and now he's on his own.
On his own in the middle of nowhere.

Can you identify with Elijah here?
Maybe you look back to the good old days, or the things you used to do, with nostalgia.
Maybe you feel frustrated because you are in such a different place now and things were really good back then.
And now you feel 'in the middle of nowhere'.
Not quite sure what you are doing, what the point of it all is. *Things are still good but I am on transition so*

Let's look at the apostle Paul:

Paul was well brought up.
He studied under the finest teacher available, Gamaliel.
Paul was a devout, religious man, who knew the Scriptures well.
Paul would have been accustomed to wealth and comfort . . . and yet he ended up poor, beaten, shipwrecked, in danger (e.g. 2 Corinthians 11:23–29).
Quite a change!

And what did Paul have to say about this change?
Philippians, 4:11:
'I have learned to be content whatever the circumstances.'

2

Day 1

Paul had *learned* to be content, whatever was going on around him – it didn't just happen!
He'd learned through spending time with God.
It's difficult to be discontented when you are spending quality time with God. – *Worship*
He'd learned through instruction, both from God and other people.
He'd spent time with other Christians and learned from them how to be content.

Are you learning from the good example of your fellow Christians? *The key to being content is*
Are they learning from you? *coming to God & being intimate with Him*

And Paul had learned to get into the *habit* of being content.
Being content had become normal for him, whatever else was happening in his life.
Habits are formed, they don't just happen.
Not many newborn babies enjoy football, but quite a few teenagers passionately support a football team every week – they get into the habit of doing so!

How do we get into the habit of being content? *Be practising thankfulness*
How can you do it?
Focus on God.
And focus, and focus, and focus until whatever else is going on around you does not matter so much.
It fades . . . and you are still content.

Paul goes on to say (Philippians 4:12):
'I know what it is to be in need, and I know what it is to have plenty. I have learned the secret of being content in any and every situation'.

Here, Paul goes further.
He expands on what he has just said –
this time, he says that he has learned the *secret* of being content.
A secret is not obvious when you don't know it!
It can seem impossible to work out until, one day, you get it.
And then it is obvious.
You work out what it is that's been missing.
And you learn to make it a habit.
You work out how to be content.

Elijah was content whatever the circumstances.
Paul was content whatever the circumstances.
Are you?

Day 1

Lord God,

Thank you that it is possible to be content.
It is possible because you make me content.
Or at least, you want to – help me to turn to you
and learn to be content.
Please teach me the secret.

Amen

Be an Elijah

Be
content

My response:

Day 2

Well, I've been camping here by the brook for a while now and the ravens actually do come and bring me bread and meat, each morning and evening. The brook is doing nicely, I drink from it whenever I want to. This is not a bad campsite!

But the prophecy has come true now – there has been no rain for ages. I was fine with the brook but now it's drying up, so it's not much use to me any more. Anyway, it's not a problem because I am moving on. God's told me to go and live in a place called Zarephath. It's a bit of a way, though. Over seventy miles, so I guess I'd better get going.

Elijah was settled by the brook.
He knew what he was doing.
The ravens brought food, he helped himself to water.
Everything was carrying on nicely . . . until the brook dried up.

The brook was a good thing.
Cool, refreshing, cleansing . . . until it dried up.

And when this place of blessing for Elijah dried up, God moved him on.

But notice something . . .
While Elijah was enjoying the water from the brook
he was not worrying about what he'd do next.
He was not thinking about his next move, and so
missing out on the present; he was living in the moment
– and God was letting him.

You know, it's OK to enjoy God's blessings.
It's OK not to be worrying!

And then, when it was time to move on, God let Elijah
know.

Sometimes, God moves us on.
Even if the place where we are is good, we are happy,
we are being blessed,
God says, 'OK, time to get going.'

And if we don't follow him, maybe the blessings we are
currently enjoying will turn a bit sour.

Imagine if Elijah had decided that he didn't want to
leave his 'campsite of blessing' and was just going to
stay put.
He would soon realize that, without God, it had become
a campsite of nothing-ness.

No water.

No blessing.

Let's look at Jesus' disciples (Luke 5:1–11):

Many of Jesus' disciples were fishermen.
Tough, weatherbeaten, good at their job, they knew about fishing.
They fished a lot, they had done for years.
And it reaped the rewards. People liked fish.

So the fishermen caught fish and they earned a living.
And everything was OK.

But one time, they'd been out in their boat, working really hard . . . and caught nothing.

Not one fish.

They must have felt tired.
They must have felt fed up.
What they normally did just wasn't working.
They didn't know why and there was nothing they could do about it.

And then Jesus comes along.
'Try throwing your net into deeper water.'
And so they did.
And they caught fish.

Before this, the disciples had been OK, happy with how their job was going.
And then, suddenly, it wasn't going well any more.

So Jesus changed their direction.
He moved them on.
He took them deeper.
And they found blessing.

A bit like Elijah – he'd been happy with the brook, and suddenly it wasn't so good. And God moved him on.

Is God moving you on?
Physically?
Emotionally?
Spiritually?

Move with him and you will find blessing.

> *Lord God,*
>
> *Moving on is hard.*
> *Sometimes, I don't want to go anywhere.*
> *I just want to stay put.*
> *But I want more blessings from you, and I know that means I need to move on.*
> *Please help me to follow your lead, wherever it takes me.*
>
> *Amen*

Be an Elijah

Move with
God

My response:

Day 3

It was a bit of a trek but I've arrived at Zarephath. I saw a widow virtually as soon as I got here. God had told me that he's arranged for a widow to feed me, so this must be her. She looks a bit poor, though. Still, God told me she'd feed me so I guess she will. I asked her for a drink of water and then some bread but I think my assessment that the widow might not have much was spot on. She went off to get the water no problem but, when I asked her for bread, too, her face fell. Apparently, she has no bread in the house. No food, actually, just a bit of flour and oil. Basically, she was planning to use the flour and oil to cook one last meal for her and her son, and that would be it.

Elijah had faith!
He's just been on a fairly long journey, arrives at his destination, looks eagerly for a woman who will have food for him . . . and sees a poor widow.
Picking up sticks. Looking a bit forlorn.
Not exactly brimming with food.
And not exactly what Elijah would have had in mind.

And yet, Elijah remembers God's promise.
The widow would feed him.

So, despite everything, he calls out in faith,
'Please give me some food and water.'

Let's look at Samuel (1 Samuel 16):

God has told Samuel that King Saul's reign is over.
It is time to anoint a new king, and God wants Samuel to
do it.
So Samuel goes where God tells him to; he goes to
Jesse, who lives in Bethlehem.

God tells Samuel that one of Jesse's sons will be the next
king so, one by one, the sons come and stand in front of
Samuel.

The eldest, Eliab, tall, strong and handsome, arrives first.
'Surely this is the one!' thinks Samuel. 'He really looks like
a king.'
But: 'No,' says God. 'I have not chosen this one.'
The next eldest comes.
'No,' says God.
And again.
And again.
Seven sons come to Samuel, and God says 'no' about
each one of them.

Samuel gets to the end of the line and still God has not
said 'yes'.
Things are looking a bit worrying now.
This is not what Samuel had expected!

But Samuel still has faith.
He has faith in what God has told him.
So he asks Jesse if he has any more sons.
And Jesse does.
He has one more.

The boy is only young.
He's a shepherd, who spends his time out in the fields with the sheep.
He's brought before Samuel . . . and God says, 'Yes.'
So Samuel anoints him as king.

During this process, when Samuel thinks to anoint one of the eldest, tallest sons of Jesse, God says to him, '[People look] at the outward appearance, but the LORD looks at the heart' (1 Samuel 16:7).

What a challenge!
God is looking right into your heart.
Seeing all the secret goings-on that no one else knows about.
Is God pleased with what he sees?

And what about how you see other people?
Do you only look on the outside?
Or do you really try to understand what is going on inside?

What about situations?
Do you take them on face value or do you look deeper, trying to see God at work in them?

Elijah trusted God to be at work in the poor widow.
Samuel trusted God to be at work in the little shepherd boy.
Where do you need to trust God to be at work?

Lord God,

Help me to look beyond appearances.
Beyond what's on the outside.
Help me to see things as you see them.
To really try to understand people and situations.
To see you at work in them.
And, Lord, please help me to do the same with myself.
Help me to see me as you see me.

Amen

Be an Elijah

Trust God to be
at work

My response:

Day 4

Poor woman, she looked so fed up and scared, really at the end of her tether. It was awful and I had to speak out. 'Don't be afraid,' I said to her. 'You'll be OK. Make some bread for you and your son, but please make a bit for me first.' Thinking about it now, I probably sounded really selfish, but I knew what was coming . . . 'God says that you will always have enough food. There will always be enough flour and oil in your containers.'

The widow's face was priceless when I told her that she'd always have enough flour and oil. Sometimes I really like delivering God's messages! I am so pleased that this woman, who has been worrying and fretting, will have food provided for her by God until the rains come again.

(Later – I've just got to add this bit in!) Great news. The widow had faith and did as I said. She made me some bread, and then some for herself and her son – this has happened for days now and she's not run out of ingredients! We all have enough food.

Wow. 'God says that you will always have enough.'

Imagine what it would have been like for the widow to hear those words.

She'd been scrimping and saving, trying to make meals out of increasingly few ingredients, worrying about what she was going to do, trying not to think about the shelves in her pantry getting barer and barer . . . and then she hears those words.
'God says that you will always have enough.'

Or, to put it another way, God says –
Don't worry about it. I will sort it.

Let's look at Abraham (Genesis 22):

Abraham is going through a pretty worrying time.
God promised him a son,
the promise finally came true,
Isaac was born
and now God has told Abraham to sacrifice him.
To kill Isaac.
Seems a strange thing to be asked to do, but Abraham is obeying.
No doubt reluctantly.
No doubt wishing it wasn't him that had been asked to do this.
No doubt trying not to think about the actual moment when he would have to take a knife to his own child.
But obeying nonetheless.

So, Abraham takes Isaac to a mountain.
He ties him up, puts him on an altar, lifts the knife . . .
and, at the very last second, an angel tells him to stop.

Abraham lets the knife drop to the ground in relief.

But what now?

God had wanted Abraham to offer a sacrifice that day, but Abraham was on the mountain with nothing to offer.

Then Abraham turns round.
And he sees a ram.
God had provided.

Abraham couldn't provide the ram.
And God stepped in.

The widow couldn't provide food.
And God stepped in.

Sometimes, we can't provide.
We can't do it on our own.
Whatever the situation may be, we just can't do it.
We are 'on the mountain with nothing to offer'.
And God steps in.

'My child, you will always have enough.'

Lord God,

I give up.
I can't do it on my own any more.
Help me to be like Abraham.
To turn away from my problems and, in doing so,
see your provision.
I know you are waiting for me to do it.
And I know you are telling me that I will always
have enough –
Please give me the courage to listen.

Amen

Be an Elijah

Let God
step in

My response:

Day 5

Well, it's some time since my last diary entry and we still haven't run out of food. But the widow's son became ill (I don't think it was food poisoning!). He'd been unwell for a few days and then finally, this morning, he died. The widow kind of blamed me for his death, actually – she asked me what I'd done to her, what I had against her and whether I, the 'man of God' had only come to point out her sins and kill her son . . .

Up until this point, the widow has not really acknowledged God, apart from that he exists (1 Kings 17:12).
She's not averse to enjoying what God provides, though – she's been eating his food for days.
And everything was going along quite happily . . . until her son died.

Something bad happened.

And suddenly, the widow acknowledges God.
She wants to know what Elijah and, by implication, God has against her that means things are going wrong in her life.

Isn't that so true of human nature?
To ignore God when things are going well, but turn to him and blame him when they aren't?

But what about when we don't ignore God when things are going well?
When we try to live our lives for him and bad things still happen?

Let's look at Job:

Job is a successful man.
He has lots of animals, lots of property, lots of servants, lots of children – in fact, he is 'the greatest man among all the people of the East' (Job 1:3).

And Job is a godly man.
He fears God and hates evil.
He regularly spends time praying and worshipping God.

So, Job has a pretty good life.

And then something bad happens . . .

In the course of one day, Job loses most of his animals and servants to attackers, and then he loses his children through natural disaster.
Later, Job himself is struck down with terrible illness.

His wife taunts him, challenging him to give up on a God who would allow all these disasters to happen . . . and what does Job say?

'Shall we accept good from God, and not trouble?' (Job 2:10)
Perhaps the key to Job being able to 'accept' trouble from God lies in the fact that he accepted good from God.
Job's life, up until now, had been really good, full of blessings.
And Job had thanked God for them.

Basically, Job was in the habit of living in such a way that he constantly remembered God and, as a result, he was used to consciously living in God's presence. He was used to sharing his day-to-day life with God.

Job knew God and, therefore, Job had his experiential knowledge of God to draw on when things got tough. And that experiential knowledge told him that God does not change.
So the God who had been there for him in the good times would be there in the tough times, too.

'From everlasting to everlasting you are God' (Psalm 90:2).

From everlasting to everlasting, and all that lies in between, God is God.

Beginning, middle and end . . . God.
The answer to every question . . . God.
The one who never leaves you . . . God.
The one who laughs with you, and cries with you . . . God.
The one who never gives up on you (even when you do) . . . God.

Where Are You?

When all around is dark, I ask, where are you?
When everything in life is hard, where are you?
When I try until I cry
and need answers to my 'whys'
where are you?

My child, I'll never leave you, I'll never turn away
I love you more than you can ever know.

In your darkness I'm your light,
when life's hard I'll be your strength.
When you try – you're not alone, I'm with you all the way.
I'm stronger than your fears
I'm the one who'll dry your tears.
Your whys are in my hands – share them with me.

My child, I'll never leave you, I'll never turn away
I love you more than you can ever know.

Lord God,

Sometimes, I don't understand.
I feel as though I have more questions than answers.
Thank you that you are good with questions.
Help me to share my 'whys' with you.
From everlasting to everlasting, you are *God.*

Amen

Be an Eijah

God is
God

My response:

Day 6

Had I come to kill her son? Well, of course I hadn't come to kill her son! I am trying not to mind about that accusation – after all, grief sometimes makes people speak in the heat of the moment. So I bit my tongue and told the widow to give her son to me.

Have you ever been falsely accused? Maybe you've tried to speak or act with sincere motives but been accused of negative intentions, of being malicious/dishonest/self-seeking?

This is the situation in which Elijah finds himself in his diary entry today.
And killing someone is a pretty big thing to be accused of!

But notice that Elijah does not retaliate.
He doesn't get into an argument with the widow and try to point out how wrong and unfair she's being.
He doesn't even respond to her accusations.
Instead, he focuses on the matter in hand – the widow's dead son.
Basically, he says, 'This is not about me right now.'

Elijah recognizes that the widow is speaking in the heat
of the moment;
a very distressing moment.
Elijah looks deeper and sees that she probably doesn't
really mean what she's saying. And, in any case, Elijah
knows that what she's accusing him of is not true.
And God knows that it's not true.
Which is enough for Elijah.
There's no need for him to get all wound up about it.

And when you find yourself in a similar situation, find
yourself being wrongly blamed, there's no need to get
wound up about it . . . but that doesn't mean it's easy.
So, how can you do it?

How can you manage not to retaliate, not to argue back?

Well, one way is to remember that God knows the truth.
Another thing is to remember what Jesus said in
Matthew 22:37:

The religious leaders are aware of Jesus.
They are aware that he has been talking to and teaching
the people.
They are aware that the people really listen to him.
And the leaders don't like this.
They don't like it one bit.
After all, they are used to being the ones that the people
listen to, that the people come to, that the people are
amazed by.

So a group from the leaders (the Pharisees) decide to go and test Jesus with a question –
'Which is the greatest commandment?'

The Pharisees are quite used to this kind of thing; they often tried to distinguish which laws were more important than others.
But what about Jesus? Would he be equal to the challenge?

Well, yes! Yes, he was. And this is what he said:
'Love the Lord your God with all your heart and with all your soul and with all your mind.'

Let's apply this commandment to the question of not retaliating:

'Love the Lord your God with all your heart and soul and mind.'

What does this mean in actuality?
Well, I think it means to be all-consumed with God.
To be full-to-the-brim with God.

And, if you are full-to-the-brim with God, there won't be room for things such as lashing out and retaliating.
But isn't it easy, especially in the heat of the moment, to not be full of God but instead to be full, or partially full, of self?
To shove God out?

Day 6

And that's when the trouble starts . . .

I remember being told when I was a child, to 'count to ten'.
If I was angry, retaliating, arguing – 'Count to ten before you speak.'
I guess this was to make me calm down, to stop and think about what I was going to say.
I have to admit that I no longer count to ten, but I do try to remember to bring God into the situation.
Remember to bring God into my heart and into my soul and into my mind.
Remember to love him.
And when I remember how much I love him, I don't want to hurt him by lashing out at other people . . .

So I suppose that now, instead of counting to ten, my mantra when faced with false accusations and being tempted to lash out, is:
'I love God, I love God, I love God . . .'

Try it!

Lord God,

I want you to be number one in my life.
Number one in my relationships with others.
Help me to be so full-to-the-brim with you that I
automatically bring you into every situation.
Help me to realize that it's not all about me.
I love you, Father.
I love you, I love you, I love you . . .

Amen

Be an Elijah

It's not all
about me

My response:

Day 7

As I say, I told the widow to give her son to me. To be fair, she did give him to me, straight away, so I guess she must trust me. I took the boy upstairs to my bedroom and put him on the bed. So, there was this dead boy lying on my bed . . . what to do next? I did the only thing I could do – I cried out to God: 'What on earth is going on? Have you really caused this terrible thing to happen to the widow I am staying with?' Then I lay down on top of the boy and asked God to bring him back to life.

Despite her lashing out at Elijah earlier, the widow must have really trusted him.
She gave the biggest thing in her life to him.
She must have spent so much time thinking about her son: worrying about what she'd feed him, then worrying about him being ill, then watching him die.
The widow had invested a lot in her son.
And she'd been the only one around, she'd borne all the worry by herself, with no one to share it.

Yet, rather than hold on to her son, she gives him to Elijah.
She lets go.

She lets Elijah take him away, take him upstairs –
and she does not follow him.
She doesn't need to know what Elijah is going to do,
or how he's going to do it.
It is enough for her to know that Elijah is dealing with it.

How about you?
With that worry or problem or concern that you can't
get out of your head?
You go over and over it – getting nowhere but not able
to let it go.

What about giving it to God?

And when I say giving it to God, I don't mean handing it
over for a couple of minutes, then snatching it back and
starting to worry about it all over again!

I mean by following the widow's example, by letting go
and letting God take it 'upstairs'.

Letting him deal with it.

And then not worrying about how he is dealing with it.

Let it be enough that he is.

Solomon, in Proverbs 23:26a, said, 'My son, give me your
heart'.

Hear God, ever so gently, saying those words to you –
'My son, my daughter, give me your heart.'

Give me your troubles, your worries,
your seemingly unsolvable problems,
things you think are buried but aren't.

Give me *all* the things that are on your heart.

You don't have to bear them alone.
Let go of them.
Give them to me.
Leave them with me.
Let me deal with them.

Give me your heart.

Jesus said (Matthew 11:28):
'Come to me, all you who are weary and burdened, and I
will give you rest.'

Are you tired?
Are you loaded down?

Come to Jesus.
Give things to him and he will give you rest.

Not 'might' give you rest.
Not 'will consider' giving you rest.

Come to Jesus and he *will* give you rest.

Lord God,

Help me to give things to you.
I have so many worries and concerns that I hold
on to – help me to let go.
Thank you that you are there.
Thank you that you offer me rest.
Please, Lord, help me to give you my heart.

Amen

Be an Elijah

Give God
my heart

My response:

Day 8

Well, to cut a long story short, the widow's son is alive and well. God heard my prayer and brought him back to life. I carried him downstairs and gave him to his mum. 'Look,' I said to her. 'Look! Your son is alive.' To say that the widow was overjoyed would be an understatement. She was absolutely thrilled to have her son back. God is good! ☺ The widow said that she now realizes that I really do follow God and that what he does and says through me is true – good day all round.

How fantastic! God brought the widow's son back to life. But isn't it interesting that Elijah had to tell her to look? Even though she was actually holding her son, it's almost as though she doesn't dare to look.
Doesn't dare hope that her son really is alive.
She's given her son's body to Elijah, left it with him, expected him to deal with it and, now that he has, she doesn't dare check to see the result.

If Elijah hadn't told her to look, she'd have missed out on something amazing.
Just imagine if she'd never actually looked at her son – she would not know that he was alive! She would miss

out on the joy, miss out on the excitement of this miracle.
What might you be missing out on because you don't
look?
God is at work all around you, in every aspect of your
life, but if you don't look, you won't see it.
Live with expectation, expectation that you will see God
at work, in big things and small.
Because he *is* at work!
And you don't want to miss it . . .

This story is found in 1 Kings 17, and verse 22 says, 'the
boy's life returned to him, and he lived.'
Why add 'and he lived' after saying that he had come
back to life?
It seems an unnecessary addition.

Let's look at Ezekiel 37:
God has given Ezekiel the job of prophesying to God's
disobedient people.
Ezekiel faithfully tells them the messages that God gives
him.

One day, God whisked Ezekiel away and placed him in a
valley.
A valley which was full of dry bones.
God told Ezekiel to speak to the bones and tell them to
come to life.
So Ezekiel did.
And, as he watched, the bones came together. They
attached themselves to each other as skeletons and

then flesh, tendons and skin covered them.
So there they were, these bodies, all put together
perfectly – except for one thing. There was no breath in
them.

God told Ezekiel to prophesy again.
To tell breath to come into the bodies.

And breath did enter them.
They stood, each and every one.
They rose up and formed a vast army.
They lived.

But what was the point of all this?
Well, God explained it to Ezekiel . . .

He said that, basically, the bones represented God's
people, the Israelites.
The Israelites were fed up, suffering, without hope,
feeling cut off from God, ready to give up and die.
A bit like the bones when they were put together – the
bodies were there but there was no breath in them, no life.

But, God said, I will bring the Israelites back to life.
I will open the graves that they are prematurely burying
themselves in.
I will raise them up.
Up from the depression and despair that they've sunk
into.
I will put my Spirit in them . . . *and they will live.*

41

What about you?

Do you feel that you exist but aren't really living?

You function day to day but often feel depressed and fed up, with no sense of joy or purpose?

Let God breathe his Spirit over you.

Into you.

Into every aspect of your life and of your living.

The bones received God's breath and went from merely 'being there' to really living.

To being an army.

They had a God-given purpose and they lived it.

Are you living your God-given purpose?

The widow's son was brought back to life and he lived. We don't know what his long-term God-given purpose was, but you can be sure that he had one.

The bones knew their long-term purpose,

the boy didn't.

Sometimes we know our purpose, sometimes we don't know it yet – but it is exciting finding out!

The bones' purpose was to be raised up as an army, their future was mapped out.

The boy's purpose was to come back to life that day.

Sometimes God's purposes for us are long-term but sometimes they are for today.

What has God purposed for you today?

Day 8

Lord God,

Sometimes, I go around with my eyes closed.
I miss out on seeing you at work.
Help me to open my eyes.
To see what you are doing, and to see what you
want me to do.
What you have purposed for me.
Help me to listen when you tell me to look!

Amen

Be an Elijah

Live God's
purpose

My response:

Day 9

God spoke to me again today. It seems ages since his word came to me. The last time was when he told me to come to Zarapheth, and that was years ago. I've been here a long time. Just to clarify, I don't mean that God hasn't been speaking to me while I've been here. He has, but just not with such specific instructions as he gave me today – he wants me to go and see King Ahab again. God is going to send rain!

Remember back in Elijah's first diary entry?
When God said that there would be no rain?
Well, there hasn't been, right up until now!
And don't forget, Elijah has been staying with the widow for a while.
So he had not really heard instructions from God about what to do next for a long time.
What was going on?

Had God forgotten about him?

Let's look at Psalm 13, which David wrote:

How long, O Lord? Will you forget me for ever?
How long will you hide your face from me?

Here, David is feeling forgotten by God – and he tells him so.
And that's OK.
It's OK for him to be honest with God.

And it's OK for you, too.

*How long must I wrestle with my thoughts and every day
have sorrow in my heart?
How long will my enemy triumph over me?*

David is feeling alone.
He's feeling sorry for himself.
He's wrestling and sorrowing.
And he seems to forget that he doesn't have to wrestle
and sorrow alone.

It's an easy thing to do.
When we are struggling or sorrowing, we think that no
one understands.
That we have got to go through it all alone.
We almost become a martyr to our own cause.

And we forget that we have a God who understands,
a God who is right there.

*Look on me and answer, O Lord my God.
Give light to my eyes, or I will sleep in death;*

Now David demands that God looks at him,
he demands God's attention.

But David is wasting his breath!
God is already looking at him, already paying him attention.
Just as he is with you.
But David is too down in the dumps to notice.

Are you?

my enemy will say, 'I have overcome him,'
And my foes will rejoice when I fall.

And then David starts worrying about what other
people think.
He's made demands of God, but he has not actually
stopped to consider God's thoughts about his situation.
Ironically, though, he worries plenty about what other
people think!

Surely that is getting his priorities wrong.
What are *God's* thoughts about his current situation
would be a better thing to focus on.
In fact, God's thoughts are always the best thing to
focus on . . .

But I trust in your unfailing love;
my heart rejoices in your salvation.

The key word here is 'But'.
Despite all that is going on – feeling far from God, not
sure God cares or notices him, worried about what other
people think, David can say 'But'.

Bad stuff is happening right now BUT I trust in the love of God, I rejoice in what he has done for me.
I don't understand what is going on BUT I trust in the love of God.
I don't 'feel the love' right now BUT I trust in the love of God.

I will sing to the Lord,
for he has been good to me.

Nothing has changed circumstantially since the beginning of the psalm, and yet David has gone from thinking that God has abandoned him to bursting into song because God has been so good to him!
What?!

Light shows up best in darkness.
David needed the dark times to show off God's light.
And David used them to do just that.

David acknowledged that things were tough.
Acknowledged that he was struggling.
And he could still say BUT I trust in God's love.

How do you use your dark times?

> *Lord God,*
>
> *Help me to remember to say 'But' . . .*
>
> *Amen*

Be an Elijah

BUT I trust in
God's love

My response:

Day 10

I was on my way to see King Ahab when you'll never guess who I bumped into – Obadiah! Obadiah is in charge of Ahab's palace and he is a really devout man. Once, he even defied Queen Jezebel, who was killing the Lord's prophets, by hiding the prophets in a cave. It was so good for me to see another believer! Obadiah told me that King Ahab is desperate. Because there is no rain, animals are dying. He wants to check the whole land to see if there is at least some grass that may keep the animals alive. That's why Obadiah is here – Ahab has taken some of the land, Obadiah has taken the rest, and they are searching for grass.

We don't know very much about Obadiah but we do know that a) he worked for King Ahab, who was an idol worshipper and b) Obadiah was a devout believer in God.

So, in effect, Obadiah was a Christian who worked in a secular environment.
Like many Christians today.

I wonder whether Obadiah ever thought that it would be so much easier to follow God, if he didn't have to go

to work (or do the shopping/school run etc.) in a place
where no one else believed.
Easier to be a believer if he didn't have to be surrounded
by the jokes and comments of his colleagues.
Jokes that went against his principles as someone who
followed God.

Let's look at Mark 5:1–20:

It is a story about a man possessed by evil spirits, who
lived in the tombs near the Sea of Galilee. The man
would spend night and day crying out and cutting
himself with stones. People tried to chain him down, but
he was so strong that he simply tore the chains apart.

Enter Jesus.
Jesus commanded the evil spirits to come out of the
man, and they did.
They left the man and he was healed.
The people from the town found the man 'sitting there,
dressed and in his right mind'. And they were afraid.
They couldn't understand what had happened.
So they begged Jesus to leave their region.

As Jesus was getting into his boat to leave, the man who
had been possessed by evil spirits came up to him.
'Please, let me come with you.'

You can see the man's point.
Better to stay with Jesus and be surrounded by him and

his disciples all the time than by people who had tried to chain him up!

But Jesus says no.
No.
Instead, go back to your family, friends and neighbours and tell them about what's happened.
Yes, even the ones who tried to chain you up.
Tell them what I have done for you.
Go to them and let them see by your life that you've been changed, that you are different.

Live your life among them but live it for me.

We know that Obadiah knew Elijah – he recognized him when they saw each other.
So Obadiah knew that Elijah worked full-time for God.
Elijah wasn't automatically surrounded, day in, day out, by people 'at the office' who didn't share his beliefs.

Maybe Obadiah thought that Elijah had it easy?
Wished he could do what Elijah did.
But Obadiah wasn't Elijah, and Elijah wasn't Obadiah.

They each had different *but equally important* things to do –
equally important lives to live for God.

Maybe you're in a situation you want to get out of?
A situation that makes it hard to be a Christian?

Day 10

If only there were more Christians around you, things would be so much easier?
Or, if only you had someone else's life, things would be fine.
Everything always works out better for other people.

Maybe God is saying to you, actually, you are right where I need you to be.
So stop comparing.
You are just who I need you to be.

Live your life exactly where you are,
in the situations and circumstances you are in,
and live it for me.

Lord God,

It is so easy to compare.
To compare myself to others and to think they have it easy.
Or that I don't match up.
Help me to remember that you created me.
That you made me just what you want me to be.
And that you don't make comparisons.
I want to live the life you've given me –
and live it for you.

Amen

Be an Elijah

Live for
God

My response:

Day 11

Obadiah could hardly believe it was me! But I managed to convince him in the end, and asked him to go and tell Ahab that I am here.

   You'd have thought I'd asked him to cut off his own hand or something – he started babbling, and saying he'd hidden 100 prophets, and worrying, and saying Ahab would kill him. I only asked him to tell Ahab I am here! Obadiah works with Ahab so I thought he'd be seeing him before long anyway. But eventually I managed to persuade Obadiah that I would not get him into trouble by doing a disappearing act. I really would wait and see Ahab. So Obadiah went and passed on the message to Ahab, who came to meet me.

Haven't I done enough? Isn't it someone else's turn now?
This seems to be what Obadiah is saying.
He'd faithfully followed God and he'd hidden and protected 100 of the Lord's prophets.
Surely that was enough to be going on with?
It looks as though Obadiah might be patting himself on the back here.

It can be easy to be like Obadiah, can't it?

To look at something wonderful you did yesterday, last week, last year, ten years ago . . . and still try to live in the light of it.

Yes, it probably was a wonderful thing that happened; you really served God.

And that's great.

It's important to recognize and enjoy the victories that God gives you.

But it is equally important to move on.

God will have another job, another victory in store!

In the end, Obadiah was persuaded to keep looking for victories.

And his task this time was to pass on a message to Ahab.

Pass on a message.

It might not seem like much but it was a vital job.

To take a message from Elijah straight to the king.

It was a message that the king needed to hear.

A message that Obadiah could pass on.

And he did.

And so Obadiah had another victory.

Sometimes, we may feel that God does not have much for us to do.

We see other people having victories for God all over the place, and yet we don't seem to have the opportunity or ability.

But think about it . . . what was Obadiah's victory?
Pass on a message.
Pass on a message to the king on behalf of Elijah.

What 'messages' can you deliver to God on behalf of others?
Elijah was in a situation where he needed to see the king, and Obadiah was in the position to pass on the message.

Let's look at Peter, in Acts 12:1–19:

King Herod was arresting Christians, which is why Peter found himself in jail.
One night, an angel appeared in the prison and led Peter to freedom and safety.
That's one side of the story, anyway – this is the other:

A group of people have met together in a house.
They have not met merely to socialize.
They have met because they have a mission.
And their mission is to pray for Peter.
Peter was in need and these people faithfully 'passed on the message' to God.
And so Peter found freedom.

What situation are people around you in?
What do they need from God?
You are in the position to pass on the message.

In his letter to the Thessalonian church (which was having a hard time), Paul tells the Christians that he constantly prays for them.

What about people around you who are struggling? Can you, like Paul, assure them of your prayers? Assure them that you are passing messages to God on their behalf?

Lord God,

There is so much hurt in the world.
Thank you that you do care.
Help me to be your messenger.
When I see people struggling, help me to pray for them.
Help me remember to pass on messages to you.

Amen

Be an Elijah

Pass God
messages

My response:

Day 12

I've been remembering about when the widow blamed me for the death of her son, because now Ahab is blaming me for the tough spot he is in – what is it about me?! Ahab came up to me, and the first thing he did was blame me for all Israel's troubles. I thought that was a bit rich, coming from the king who had abandoned God's ways and started worshipping other gods . . . and I told him so. I did 'look deeper' first, as I did with the widow, but whereas the widow was coming from a place of hurt and bewilderment, Ahab was just trying to wriggle out of the blame he knew he deserved.

Trying to wriggle out of the blame is often our default mode, isn't it?
It's not my fault!
Don't blame me!
Look at what you've done now!
It wasn't me, it was him!

Ahab is wriggling here.
He is trying to blame everything that has gone wrong on Elijah, rather than face the truth.

Let's look at Adam and Eve:

Adam and Eve live in a beautiful garden.

They are basically allowed to do whatever they want, except eat fruit from one particular tree.

But, one day, Eve does eat fruit from the forbidden tree.

And she gives some to Adam, who eats it too.

Later, God asks Adam outright:

'Did you eat fruit from the tree I told you not to eat from?'

And Adam tries to shift the blame –

'It is really Eve's fault. Don't blame me! I only ate it because she gave it to me.'

As a result of eating the fruit, God says to Adam that he will have to work hard on the land to produce any good crops (crops had been freely provided for him before now).

And why would Adam have to do this?

'Because *you* listened to your wife and ate'

(Genesis 3:17, my emphasis).

Just as Elijah did with Ahab, God gets straight to the heart of the matter.

Adam, I'm not interested in excuses.

The fact is that you chose to eat the fruit.

Adam was making excuses to God.

Maybe because he was afraid of the consequences of his actions.

Maybe because he didn't want to admit that he'd disobeyed God.

Maybe because he was scared of God's anger.
Maybe because he didn't want to lose face in front of his wife.
Whatever the reason, he made excuses.

'Nothing in all creation is hidden from God's sight' (Hebrews 4:13).
Adam was part of creation – every part of him.
You are part of God's creation – every part of you.

What you do, what you say, what you think, who you are.
Nothing about you is hidden from God.

So there is no point in trying to hide things!
No point in pretending.
No point in abdicating responsibility.
No point in making excuses.

Better to just be honest with God – and remember, he loves you *no matter what*.

'Do not conform any longer to the pattern of this world, but be transformed by the renewing of your mind' (Romans 12:2).

We live in an 'avoid blame at all costs' world.
We make excuses for ourselves and to ourselves.
That's not how God intended things to be.
He values honesty.

And, as we take to heart this verse in Romans, we will conform less and less to this world, which will mean that we will have fewer and fewer reasons to make excuses anyway!

Lord God,

I am a master at making excuses.
I know I am.
Help me to be honest with myself.
And to be honest with you.
Thank you that you know me inside out.
You know all my fears and failings . . .
and yet you love me anyway.

Amen

Be an Elijah

Don't make
excuses

My response:

Day 13

I can't believe the audacity of Ahab, blaming me! So
I decided we'd better have it out. I told Ahab to get all
the people together, including the 450 prophets of Baal
and Asherah, the 'gods' that Ahab has introduced to
Israel. So he did and we all met together on Mount
Carmel.

So, Ahab is busy accusing Elijah and, rather than simmer
and seethe with anger, Elijah decides that the best
course of action is to get things out in the open.

It can be easy to let things go over and over in our
minds rather than dealing with them, can't it?
Particularly if they relate to another person.

Most of us know people (or maybe are people) who
have an ongoing feud with their family or friends. Often,
people who were formerly extremely close have not
spoken to one another for years.
And why?
Well, the irony is that many people in this situation can't
actually remember what the disagreement was about.
Or if they can, it is no longer relevant.

Let's look at Jacob and Esau, Genesis 27:
Jacob and Esau were twins. Esau was the elder by moments.
As they grew up, it became apparent that the boys had
very different interests.
Esau enjoyed hunting and being out in the open fields,
while Jacob was quieter, preferring to stay at home.

One day, when the twins' father, Isaac, was very old,
he wanted to bless his elder son, Esau, before he died.
So he called Esau to him and asked him to prepare a
favourite dish. The plan was that after eating it, Isaac
would bless Esau.
So off Esau went, to catch some game for the meal.

Meanwhile, the twins' mother, Rebekah, had overheard
the conversation between Isaac and Esau. And Rebekah
wanted her favourite son, Jacob, to receive the blessing
instead of Esau. So she quickly concocted a plan of her
own – Jacob would pretend to be Esau.
Rebekah cooked Isaac's favourite meal, covered Jacob's
hands and neck with animal skins (Esau was a hairy
man, Jacob wasn't), dressed Jacob in Esau's clothes –
and off Jacob went to his father, pretending to be Esau.

And Jacob did deceive Isaac.
Jacob received the blessing that Isaac intended for Esau.

When Esau found out, he was not best pleased, to say
the least.
In fact, he was so angry that Jacob had to flee for his life.

Day 13

He fled to his uncle, where he stayed for twenty years.
Eventually, Jacob heads for home, still nervous about
what Esau might do to him – and Esau welcomes him
with open arms.
Not only that, but Esau does not refer at all to the
incident that had happened all that time ago.

Esau was over it, whereas Jacob was not and, by
implication, hadn't been for the past twenty years. Jacob
was still worrying about what his brother would do to
him, just as he had been twenty years ago.
Nothing had changed for Jacob.

Jacob was the one who had cut himself off – if he'd
stayed in touch with Esau, he'd know that Esau had
moved on.
But Jacob hadn't stayed in touch.
And so he didn't know.
So he didn't move on.
Oh, he may have appeared to – he had accumulated
great wealth, got married, had children – but inside, the
issue with his brother was still there.
And it didn't need to be.
If Jacob had dared to bring things out into the open
with Esau, he wouldn't have wasted so long worrying
needlessly.
Esau was over it!

Don't let resentment build up and simmer inside you.
Get things out in the open.

Talk to people.
A bit like a sticking plaster coming off – it may hurt, but if you do it quickly, it will cause less pain in the long run.

Lord God,

It's amazing how things can blow up.
They go round and round in my mind until they are probably way out of proportion.
But it is really hard to stop that from happening.
Help me to have the courage to get things out in the open.
To allow myself to be vulnerable.
To communicate with people – and to deal with things.

Amen

Be an Elijah

Deal with things

My response:

Day 14

When everyone had arrived, I went over to speak to them. I had a question for them – basically, how long would they sit on the fence? Wavering between God and Baal, faithful to neither? I challenged them to decide and then stick with their decision!

And guess what they said in reply? Absolutely nothing.

So, as I said yesterday, I decided to have this out. I decided to challenge the Baal worshippers to a bit of a competition. My challenge was this: prepare an altar, ready to offer a sacrifice on, but don't light it. I'd do the same. Then see whose god could start a fire. Which god could simply 'zap' flames on to the altar. Basically, whichever did would be the true God. And the people accepted my challenge (and I do mean 'people' plural – there is only one of me, but lots of them!).

Will you make up your mind?!

The people of Israel seem to find themselves in a bit of a dilemma here – which god should they follow? So they are just flitting between gods, sometimes following the true God and sometimes following the pagan god, Baal.

Day 14

Does this ring a bell with you? Not necessarily flitting between God and Baal but maybe flitting between God and material things – your house/car/computer? Or flitting between God and your professional status? Or flitting between God and money? Or flitting between God and . . . ?

Let's look at Joshua 24:

Joshua, leader of the Israelites, is nearing the end of his life. He calls all the tribes of Israel to him so that he can deliver his final speech.
He reminds them of all that God has done for them – freeing them from Egypt, protecting them in the desert, helping them conquer their enemies, giving them a land to live in.

And now Joshua's challenge is this – throw away the false gods that your ancestors worshipped.
It seems that the people, despite all that God had done for them so far, were still hanging on to other gods.
Maybe they were not actively worshipping these other gods, were not actively relying on them.
But they were hanging on to them. Just in case.

Joshua's advice is good – get rid of them! You don't need a backup plan with God.

The same is true for us today.
The things and ways that we hang on to from our old life, just in case – get rid of them!

The things we accumulate and don't let go of, just in case – get rid of them!
There's no need for a backup plan with God.

And then Joshua issues a further challenge – make your mind up.
Don't sit on the fence.
Choose who or what your god will be.

If, he says, *if* following these foreign gods is what you want, OK.
That's up to you.
'But as for me and my household, we will serve the LORD.' (v. 15)

Basically, Joshua says, I've made my mind up on this and I will not be swayed by what you do.

Can you say that?
Can you say, I will follow God, regardless of what others around me do?

And the people decide to choose God.
So Joshua gets a large stone and sets it up as a witness to the people's decision.
Whenever they saw that stone, the people would be reminded that they'd chosen to follow God.
Maybe they'd be in the market, get knocked into roughly by someone, start to lash out . . . and glance up and see the stone.

And remember – they'd chosen God.
They'd chosen God's ways.
And they'd decide not to lash out after all.

Do you have a witness between the agreement you made to follow God and his ways? Maybe a piece of jewellery, a magnet on the fridge, a sticker on the car . . . whatever it may be, have something that reminds you, throughout the day and all that the day brings, that you are following God and his ways.

Lord God,

I do choose you.
At least, I want to.
I am sorry for the times when other things seem to take over
but I do want to choose you.
Help me to remember to do so, every day.

Amen

Be an Elijah

Choose
God

My response:

Day 15

I thought I may as well let them go first. So they prepared the bull that was given to them and put it on the altar. Then they called on Baal to answer them, to send fire. Nothing. So they shouted louder and danced around. Still nothing. This went on all morning. I have to confess that I began to make fun of them a bit at this point – well, make fun of their 'god' anyway. I told them to shout louder in case he was asleep or busy or travelling! Then they shouted even louder and slashed and cut themselves in their frenzy – but still nothing. They carried on all the way into the evening, but there was still nothing from Baal.

Well, one thing that the prophets of Baal could not be faulted on was their enthusiasm! They absolutely believed, 100 per cent, in what they were doing.

Let's look at Saul, Acts 9:1–31:

Saul is a Jew through and through. He has been brought up to follow the law to the letter. And now he is an adult, he has made it his life's mission to ensure that other people follow the Jewish law, too. Ensure that other people obey the writings of the Old Testament to the nth degree, follow it absolutely.

But the problem for Saul is that Jesus came along. He showed people another way to follow the law, a new way of following God – and people really bought into it. So much so that despite Jesus no longer being around, and despite intense persecution from people such as Saul, people are still following God the Jesus way.

Saul's latest tactic has been to obtain letters from the high priest, demanding that anyone who follows Jesus be thrown into prison.
So now Saul is on his way to find these people.
He is heading for the synagogues in Damascus and, just as he nears the end of the journey, a bright light flashes around him, and he falls to the ground.

A voice speaks to him; 'Saul, why are you persecuting me?'
'Who are you?' asks Saul.
The answer? 'I am Jesus.'
And the next thing we know, Saul has become as zealous for Jesus as he was formerly against him.

'I am Jesus.'

That was enough for Saul.
He met Jesus and he followed him.

The world today is full of people who, to a greater or lesser degree than Saul, are against Jesus.
But have they *met* Jesus?
Saul had met, or had contact with, lots of people who followed Jesus.
But he hadn't met Jesus.

Today, many churches hold social get-togethers and outreach events for non-Christians to come to.
And the guests come, and are made very welcome, and have a good time, and meet people who follow Jesus . . .
and then disappear from church life until the next event.

Why?
Could it be possible that, in being so keen to be friendly and welcoming, we forget to introduce people to Jesus?

People need to meet Jesus.
Let's not be so enthusiastic to simply get people into church that we forget to introduce them to Jesus.

The prophets of Baal sincerely believed that they were zealous for the right thing, the right god, but they were wrong.
Saul sincerely believed that he was zealous for the right thing, but he was wrong.

We must make sure that we are putting our zeal, our energies, our time into the right thing. And what could be more right than introducing Jesus?

Lord God,

Help me to introduce Jesus and not merely 'Jesus Events'.
In my enthusiasm to be welcoming, don't let me forget the main point –
meeting Jesus.

Amen

Be an Elijah

Introduce
Jesus

My response:

Day 16

OK, they'd had their turn and now it was over to me. The first thing I did was to repair the altar of the Lord – it was lying in ruins! Using twelve stones, one for each tribe, I built it in the name of the Lord.

I dug a trench round the altar and arranged wood and meat on top of it. Then I had water poured on it, three times. The water was all over it, running down the sides, filling the trench around the altar.

So, now it is Elijah's turn. We might expect him to go out, guns blazing, calling down fire from heaven. He knows that God can do it and he's been waiting impatiently to prove it. Now his time has come . . . and what is the first thing he does?
Elijah repairs the altar of the Lord.
Because the altar of the Lord was in ruins and needed repairing.

Elijah did not let the task in hand make him lose sight of what was ultimately important – worshipping God.
On the one hand, Elijah was expecting a great victory from God and, juxtaposed with that, the altar of the Lord was lying in ruins.

We can apply this picture to our Christian lives.
How often does one aspect of our faith seem to be
thriving while another is lying in ruins, needing to be
repaired?
For example, maybe we go regularly to a Bible study
group but harbour anger and resentment towards a
friend or neighbour.

Let's look at Matthew 23:

Jesus is talking about the religious leaders of his day –
and he calls them 'whitewashed tombs'.
Basically, they looked good on the outside; they played
the part of being devout and faithful very well. But
inside they were full of wickedness and deceit.
A bit like a tomb that looked good from the outside but
inside was full of dead bones.

We need to make sure that we don't become a
whitewashed tomb – simply playing the part on the
outside.
It can be easy to get into a bit of a rut in your Christian
life, can't it?
To go through the motions of church, home groups and
so on, but to actually be spiritually dead inside.
But you can't do that forever . . .
And, anyway, spiritually dead is not a nice way to be!

The crucial thing is to keep a close relationship with God.
Look after the 'inside' and the 'outside' will take care of

itself – not the other way round.
'Out of the overflow of the heart the mouth speaks'
(Matthew 12:34).

So, what is inside is reflected on what is outside.
We need to concentrate on having hearts and minds
that are set apart for God, not lying in ruins.
And, if they are in ruins, repair them.
Make it a priority – there is nothing that is more
important.

Lord God,

*When I look at my 'outside' and my 'inside,' they
often don't match up.
And I know it is the inside that needs working on.
Please work with me.
I want my heart to have a good overflow!*

Amen

Be an Elijah

Don't be a
whitewashed
tomb

My response:

Day 17

Then, when it was time for my sacrifice, I stepped forward – all eyes were on me. And I prayed. I asked God to prove that he is God. To show every person there, beyond a shadow of a doubt, that he is sovereign. Then I acknowledged what he has done – after all, everything I've done has only happened because he commanded me to do it!

During his prayer, Elijah acknowledges what God has done; he says: 'I am your servant and have done all these things at your command' (1 Kings 18:36).

Notice that although Elijah has literally been the one to do things, he gives the glory to God. He only did what God told him to do.

And we need to remember to do the same.
But sometimes it can be easy to slip into wanting the credit and glory for ourselves.

Let's look at Daniel:

Daniel has been taken from his home to the court of King Nebuchadnezzar. He is trying to stay faithful to

God, to live God's way, despite being in a foreign place. Despite being surrounded by people who don't live God's way.

And then, one night, the king has a disturbing dream. In the morning, he calls his advisors and astrologers and demands that they tell him about the dream and its meaning. If they can't, they will be put to death. In fact, all the wise men in Babylon will be put to death.

The advisors and astrologers are unable to interpret the dream.
As they are about to be killed, Daniel steps forward.
He asks for time to interpret the dream.
Then he goes home, calls his friends and they begin to pray.
They ask God to reveal the meaning of the dream to them and, during the night, God reveals the dream to Daniel.

So, Daniel is brought before the king.
Imagine the scene – a troubled king, worried advisors, confused servants . . .
Enter Daniel.
With the interpretation of the dream.

Basically, Daniel has a chance to save the day!
And in front of the most important people in Babylon.
This is an opportunity for Daniel to really look good.
King Nebuchadnezzar asks Daniel, 'Can you interpret the dream that I had?'

This is it! Daniel can step forward and say that yes, actually, he can.
But instead, Daniel says, 'No, I can't.'
What?

There is Daniel, standing before the king, with full knowledge of the meaning of the dream, and he says no, he can't interpret it.

'*I* can't', says Daniel. '*But* there is a God in heaven who can.'

And Daniel goes on to give God's interpretation of the meaning of the dream.
Goes on to give God glory.

Do you give God the glory?

'If anyone serves, he should do it with the strength God provides, so that in all things God may be praised' (1 Peter 4:11).

Is God praised through you?
Do your actions and words point others to him?
Or do you take the praise for yourself?

Think about your day, situations you deal with, people you meet, praise that might be directed your way. When pride sneaks up and you want the glory for yourself, remember: you can only do things because God helps.

Day 17

It is God's glory – don't steal it!

Lord God,

I just want to say sorry.
Sorry for the times I steal your glory.
I know I do it.
I know I sometimes want the glory for myself.
Thank you that you still want to use even me to reflect your glory.
Help me to reflect it, not steal it.

Amen

Be an Elijah

Don't steal
God's glory

My response:

Day 18

I carried on praying and I looked ahead to what God will do (I know he'll answer me so that everyone knows he is God). Finally I focused on what he is doing – turning people's hearts back to himself. Past, present and future, all in one prayer!

Another part of Elijah's prayer focuses on what God is doing:

'. . . you are turning their hearts back again.'

On the face of it, these people around Elijah did not appear to be having their hearts turned back to God, did they?!
They appeared to be as anti-God as possible.

Yet Elijah says in his prayer that God is turning their hearts back again.

We can take real encouragement from this.
When people seem hardened against God, it is just possible that even so God is turning their hearts.

Let's look at Ezekiel 11:

God has a message for the exiled nation of Israel, and he is giving it through Ezekiel. Basically, Israel had ignored God and his ways so God scattered them among other nations.

But now God says, 'I will bring them back.

They won't stay scattered forever.

And not only that, I will give them a new heart.'

Before, when the Israelites rejected God,

they had hearts of stone.

Now God is promising them new hearts, hearts of flesh.

He was going to turn their hearts around again,

maybe was *already* turning them!

What about your heart?

Has it strayed from God?

Maybe, to others looking on, it doesn't seem so – you seem as you always have. Committed to God, helping at church, going to Bible study . . .

But you know.

You know that your heart is no longer as 'towards' God, as tuned in to God as it used to be.

You know that it is becoming stony.

Let God bring you back.

Let him turn your heart back again.

Let him remove the stone and give you a heart of flesh.

A heart that lives and beats for him.

And not just in the big situations, but in everyday life.
When you come across people and situations,
before leaping in to the conversation
or to deal with the problem,
pause for a minute.
Consciously turn your heart towards God.
Let how you respond be a heart reflection of him.

Lord God,

Help me to trust you with other people's hearts.
And with my own.
Help me to turn towards you.
Help me to truly reflect your heart.

Amen

Be an Elijah

Reflect God's
Heart

My response:

Day 19

When I had finished praying, the fire of God came down from heaven! It burned up everything – the wood, stones, soil, even the water in the trench!
  When everyone saw this, they bowed before my God, acknowledging him to be the true God. And all the prophets of Baal were taken away and killed.

When Elijah had finished praying, God sent fire from heaven.
God could have responded before the prayer, or during the prayer, and sometimes he does . . . but this time, he responded *after* the prayer.

There is an important lesson here – don't give up with prayer.
And, secondly, don't get distracted from it . . .

Everyone around Elijah was watching.
Watching to see what would happen.
Watching to see what Elijah would do.
Watching to see what Elijah's God would do.

The pressure is on! And yet, Elijah focuses on his prayer and who he is praying to.

He does not allow what is happening around him to
interfere.

It is almost as if, for this moment, there is just God and
Elijah.

Everything else sort of fades as Elijah communes with
his God.

And Elijah finishes his prayer.

What about when you pray?

Do you find your mind wandering?

Or do you, like Elijah, become so enthralled with God
that everything else fades?

So caught up with talking to God, so focused on him,
that nothing that is going on around you will distract
you?

God is a good 'thing' to get caught up with!

So, in answer to Elijah's prayer, God sent fire from
heaven which burned up everything,
including the water.

I wonder why Elijah had decided to pour water over the
altar before God sent the fire? Probably to make it even
clearer that God is God – after all, he is a God who can
set fire to sopping wet wood!

But God goes one step further – he burns the water up,
too.

And this was more than a puddle that was burned up –
this was a trench full of water.

God is a God who exceeds our expectations.
'[God] is able to do immeasurably more than all we ask or imagine, according to his power that is at work within us' (Ephesians 3:20).

God is not limited by our finite minds and ideas – he is infinite!
His plans and ways are so much bigger and better than ours.
So trust him.

Now that the people have seen God send fire from heaven, what do they do?
They bow in worship and acknowledge God.
And why?
Because God answered Elijah's prayer.
If he hadn't, the people would not have seen his power.
And, if Elijah hadn't prayed, God would have had nothing to answer . . .

Because of Elijah's prayer, all these people, who had previously not known or recognized God, acknowledged him as God.

What will your prayers accomplish?
Do you know people who desperately need God but don't seem interested?
Pray for them.
Faithfully.
Don't give up.

Keep going.
Don't get distracted.

Finish your prayer . . . and leave the rest in God's hands.

Lord God,

The fact that I can talk to you any time I want is amazing.
You are the creator, the all-powerful God.
Lord, I want to become so wrapped up in you when I pray that everything else fades.
Thank you that I can talk to you about anything and anyone.
Help me to be faithful.
Help me not to get distracted.
Help me to give you something to answer,
and to finish my prayers.

Amen

Be an Elijah

Pray!

My response:

Day 20

*And that was that! I told Ahab to go and get
something to eat and drink – he didn't need to worry
any more, as the rain was on its way. So off he went
to get some food . . .*

Well, it's over.
God has emphatically won the contest.
So Elijah tells Ahab that he can rest easy now because
rain is coming.
And Ahab does; he goes off to relax over a meal.

As yet, Ahab has not seen even a drop of rain but, based
purely on what Elijah tells him, Ahab believes that rain is
on its way.
I doubt that Ahab would have believed just anyone who
told him – after a long time of drought with no sign of
rain – that rain was on its way.
But he believed Elijah.
Why?

Ahab had seen a bit of Elijah, on and off, over the past
few years.
He had seen him appear before the king (himself!) and
announce that there would be no rain.

He had seen Elijah refuse to bow to pressure and appear solely because Ahab had summoned him, but to come only in God's timing.

He had seen Elijah challenge the prophets of Baal and prove that God is the true God.

Ahab had seen Elijah in some quite varied situations, many of which would not have been pleasing to Ahab – so why does he have this confidence in Elijah?

Because of Elijah's consistency.

Whatever situation Elijah found himself in, his reliance on God never wavered. And that spoke volumes.

Ahab's confidence and trust in Elijah was a direct result of Elijah's confidence and trust in God.

Let's look at Daniel:

Daniel has been consistent in his witness for God.

He has refused to eat defiled food, he has interpreted dreams for the king, he has refused to pray to the king.

And, throughout, he has consistently maintained his witness, worship and trust in God.

So much so that now he finds himself surrounded by hungry lions.

The king, Darius, had reluctantly watched Daniel being thrown to the lions, had spent a sleepless night worrying about him and has now hurried back in the morning to see if Daniel is OK.

To see if Daniel's God has saved him from the lions – and he has!
Daniel is alive and well.

And this incident, on the back of Daniel's previous consistency in his trust in God, had such an impact on King Darius that he ordered everyone in his kingdom to worship and revere Daniel's God.

What about you?
Are you consistent in your confidence and trust in God?
If you are, then people will not be able to help but respect you, even if they don't like what you say or do.

Ahab respected Elijah, but Elijah had to earn that respect.
It is the same for us today – if we want people to respect us, to take our faith seriously, we need to earn that respect.
We need to be consistent, to trust in God in every situation and to show that we are trusting him . . . to tell people that we can only do things because God is with us.

Day 20

Lord God,

*Help me to trust and believe in you in every
situation, even when it's hard.
Help me to be consistent, so that people can see
from my life that you are worth trusting.*

Amen

Be an Elijah

Be
consistent

My response:

Day 21

Ahab went off but I climbed right to the top of the mountain and sat down with my face between my knees.

What has happened? Is Elijah OK?
Someone entering Elijah's story at this point might well assume that something terrible has happened,
but we know differently.
We know that Elijah has just won a tremendous spiritual victory over the false god, Baal.

So what is Elijah doing alone, on the ground, lowering his face as far as he can?
Why isn't he off celebrating with Ahab?
Boasting about his God?
Enjoying the moment of victory?

Well, it seems that Elijah wants to take stock.
Rather than stick around and enjoy the congratulations and admiration from people, including the king, Elijah wants to be alone with God and process what has happened.

Elijah doesn't want to risk losing sight of God in the midst of his victory.

But notice where he chooses to be alone with God –
on top of the mountain where he has just won spiritual
victory.
By going away by himself, Elijah is not trying to pretend
that the victory never happened.
He is not engaging in a sort of warped false modesty.
He is simply wanting to 'work through' the victory with
God.

It is important that we acknowledge when God has
worked something out through us.
And it is OK to enjoy that.
To spend time at the top of the mountain.
But, at the same time, we must remember to keep our
spiritual feet firmly on the ground.

Let's look at John 6:

Jesus has used just five loaves and two fish to feed over
five thousand people – and they all had enough to eat.
There was even some food left over!
Wow.

People must have been absolutely amazed at what
they'd seen.
In fact, they were amazed.
So amazed that they decided that the obvious thing to
do was to make Jesus king, then and there.
But Jesus knew that that was not the right thing to do;
he knew that his time had not yet come.

So, rather than stay around to enjoy all the admiration and praise from the crowd, Jesus took himself off and went up a mountain.
To enjoy this 'victory' with God alone.

Probably, the next time Jesus saw people who'd been in that crowd, the next time Elijah saw people who'd witnessed the scene on the mountain, they would have talked about it.
Maybe relived it.
Maybe remembered together what a great day it was.

But both Jesus and Elijah would have been having these conversations after they had processed what had happened with God.
After they had got things from his perspective.
After they had got his take on things.

When we have conversations, especially about big things, it is always a good idea to get God's perspective first.
If you have time beforehand to process things with God, great! But even if you don't, remember to constantly have a line to God during the conversation, constantly trying to feed back what his take on the situation is.
Constantly including his perspective in what you say and do.

Lord God,

Help me to take time out with you.
Time to take stock.
Time to regroup.
Time to get your perspective.
And help me to feed your perspective into
situations I come across.

Amen

Be an Elijah

Keep God's
perspective

My response:

Day 22

Then I told my servant to go and look towards the sea. So he did, but there was nothing there. So I told him to go and look again . . . and again . . . he went six times and saw nothing. Finally, on the seventh time, he told me that he had seen a tiny cloud rising up from the sea. So I told him to go and tell Ahab, and to hurry up about it, before the rain stopped him from going. The sky went really black, wind came . . . and then the rain. It absolutely threw it down!

Then God gave me power and helped me to run really fast. I actually ran ahead of Ahab's chariot, beating him all the way to Jezreel. I ran at least sixteen miles! I know people from Gilead are good runners but I don't think I've ever run this well before.

Elijah tells his servant to keep looking – even though, to all intents and purposes, there is nothing to see!
But Elijah knows what is coming and he doesn't want his servant to miss it.
He doesn't want his servant to look away, get distracted by other things, and miss the main event.

Maybe you have been looking.
Looking for God to step in to a particular situation.

Looking for answers to your questions.
Looking for solutions to your problems . . . and there
seems to be nothing to see.

Well, don't give up!
Keep looking.
God will be there, in his timing.
So keep looking for him, don't get distracted – you don't
want to miss him.

Let's look at Simeon (Luke 2):

Simeon was an old man.
A righteous and devout man.
A man who spent his days waiting.

Basically, Simeon was waiting for the Messiah.
The Holy Spirit had told him that he would not die
before he had seen Jesus.
Simeon would see Jesus with his own eyes!
And that is what he was waiting for,
day after day after day.

As each day drew to a close, Simeon knew that he had
not seen Jesus.
But there was always tomorrow . . . so he kept
looking.

Simeon would not be distracted from looking out for
Jesus.

Even though, day after day, there was no sign of him,
Simeon was wise enough to keep looking and wait for
God's timing.

Then, one day, Simeon went to the Temple and, at last,
this time, he saw Jesus.
And the wait was well and truly worth it.

Are you like Simeon?
Wise enough to keep looking and waiting
for God's timing?
Or do you give up too soon?

Maybe God doesn't seem to be moving as quickly as
you'd like him to, or in the direction that you'd like him
to, or in the way that you'd like him to . . . so you stop
looking.
And, when you do stop looking, you miss out on what
God has in store for you.
And what God has in store for you is his very best.
And no one can define 'best' any better than God.
Sometimes his definition doesn't seem to be the same as
ours, but we can be sure that his definition is far, far better!
And his timing is perfect.

'All the days ordained for me were written in [God's]
book before one of them came to be' (Psalm 139:16).

Look out for God.
And keep looking.

Day 22

Not only in the 'big' situations and decisions that come your way.
Keep looking in the everyday things, too.

Imagine going through your day,
but doing so with Jesus.
Looking out for him in every situation you encounter.
Wondering what he would do or say.
And trying to be like him.

Try it – and then you won't have to imagine what it's like any more.

Lord God,

Thank you that you are a God who is there.
There to be found.
A God whose timing is perfect.
Help me to keep looking for you,
even when you don't show yourself when and how I expect you to.

Amen

Be an Elijah

Look for
Jesus

My response:

Day 23

Oh no, bad news – Ahab told his wife, Queen Jezebel about all that happened, including the fact that the prophets of Baal had been killed. And she got really mad, so mad that she wants to kill me.

So I am petrified and have been running for my life, literally (good thing I am decent at running). But even I can't run forever, I had to stop in the end. I stopped in the desert, sat down under a tree and prayed that I would die. After all, what is the point of me living?

Are you good at running?
Maybe you won't be competing in the next Olympics, but could you win a gold medal for running from problems?

Elijah seems to be pretty good at both types of running. He has got rid of all company and is sitting in a desert, praying to die.

Well, at least we know that Elijah was human.
What he is experiencing here is probably familiar to most of us.

Things don't go the way we'd hoped or expected they would.

We become anxious and start withdrawing (running).
Eventually we isolate ourselves, not wanting company.
So we end up in a 'desert place,' an empty place of
nothing-ness.

And what happens when Elijah is in his empty place of
nothing-ness?
He starts thinking.

Now, thinking is not a bad thing in itself, of course; we
certainly would not get far in life without being able to
think!
But when we are alone, rundown, with our heads full of
problems, our thinking can become very negative.
Which is what happened to Elijah.

He had started running because he was worried about
losing his life.
He doesn't want to die, he wants to live!
So he runs away from those who want to kill him . . . but
he seems to forget to stop.
And then he apparently forgets why he is running in the
first place.
He forgets that he is running to save his life and decides
that instead, his life is not worth living.
His perspective has changed.

Elijah is exhausted, alone, in a desert, and he gets things
a bit out of proportion.
It seems that somewhere along his marathon, he

changes from running away from Ahab to running away from himself.
Running away from a life that he sees as not worth living.
Running away because he can not see a way forward.
Running away from what he can't do.
Running away from his perception of himself.

What is your self-perception like?

God says to you (see Isaiah 43:1–4):
Fear not, I have redeemed you.
I have summoned you by name, you are mine.
You are precious and honoured in my sight . . . and I love you.

This is God's perception of you:
Precious.
Honoured.
Loved.
Worth redeeming.

God gives you a very good reason to remember to stop running.

Lord God,

I am an Olympic champion at running from problems.
And at running from myself.
Help me to see myself, my life, as you see me . . .
and to remember to stop running.

Amen

Be an Elijah

Stop
running

My response:

Day 24

I just told God that I have had enough. Told him to take my life, that it would be best all round if I die. Then I went to sleep, expecting him to get on with it. But the next thing I knew, there was an angel telling me to get up and eat something. When I looked round, I saw there was food and drink right by me. Well, the food was there, so I thought I may as well eat it. Running makes me hungry! So I ate and drank, then lay down again. This time, I would die . . .

But it seems a man can't die in peace around here. I lay back down (again) and waited to die (again), but the angel woke me up (again) and told me to eat (again). I was about to protest that I was not hungry, I had just eaten and was now waiting to die, when I realized that actually, I was still hungry. The angel said that I needed to eat to keep my strength up, because the journey was too much for me.

So, the angel keeps coming back . . . clearly, Elijah's immediate death is not on God's agenda!
And the angel tells Elijah to eat, more than once.

Eating is not just a one-off thing, is it?
We need regular food, regular meals in order to keep

our minds and bodies healthy and functioning.
And we make sure we do eat regularly.
We don't have a one-off meal and that's it for the rest of the week!

But what about spiritually?
Do we regularly feed our spiritual minds and bodies?
Or do we think that a one-off, 'church on a Sunday' is enough to keep us spiritually healthy?

The Bible says that God's mercies are 'new every morning' (Lamentations 3:23).

Let's look at the Israelites in Exodus 16:

After years of slavery in Egypt, God has given the Israelites a miraculous escape. They are free!
And they are complaining.
They hated living in Egypt but now they are looking back with longing.
Because now they are hungry.
They are remembering the food they had to eat in Egypt and are wishing they had never left.

Basically, the Israelites decided to focus on the one thing that was negative and ignore all the positives.
They ignored the fact that they were free, that God had rescued them, that they were no longer being beaten by the slave-drivers, that they were no longer expected to work harder than is humanly possible, that they had

time to be with their families . . . they ignored all that because they felt hungry.

It is an easy thing to do, isn't it?

One thing goes wrong and suddenly difficult things from the past come creeping in and start looking actually quite inviting.

It becomes easy to start believing that they were not too bad, after all.

In fact, maybe they were quite good . . .

But God steps in.

The Israelites don't need to look back.

God deals with their problem (he's good at doing that).

God deals with it by 'raining bread from heaven' for them. Each morning, the Israelites would go out from their tents and collect enough food for the day.

Then, the next day, they would do it again . . . and there was always enough food.

God did, however, tell them specifically that they should only take enough for one day.

But some of them were not convinced that the food would be there each day.

They thought they had better save some, just in case.

And, when they did, the food they saved became mouldy.

They had to throw it away.

It was useless.

Back to the verse in Lamentations:
God's mercies are 'new every morning'.
Are you like the Israelites?
Sometimes trying to 'stock up' on God?
Maybe thinking that Sunday is enough to keep you
going spiritually for the rest of the week?

But God's mercies are new *every morning*!
Just think what you are missing out on . . .

Elijah realized that a one-off meal was not enough.
The Israelites who tried to stock up on God's blessings
missed out.
It backfired.
The food went mouldy.
Because tomorrow was another day.

God wanted to give them something new, he wanted to
give them more.
Because he is a living God!
And because he has so much to give.
And because each day is different.
And because he wanted to meet their needs each day –
just as he wants to meet yours. Do you let him?

Lord God,

Your mercies are new every morning.
Help me to look for them.
I am sorry for the times when I am in the wrong place to receive what you want to give – help me to be in the right place.
Thank you so much that you are a giving God.

Amen

Be an Elijah

God wants
to give

My response:

Day 25

The food was good! The angel was right, I just needed to take a bit of time out. Now I am feeling much better about things. I have been travelling again, forty days and nights to reach Horeb . . . and I am there! Right now! Finally. I don't need to travel through the night any more, so I've found a cave here where I can bed down.

All the hard work and travelling has paid off.
Elijah has reached his destination.
So he stops.
And he finds a cave there.

But where is 'there'?
'There' is where Elijah is, and 'there' is Horeb, the mountain of God.
So, just to be absolutely clear, Elijah finds refuge in a cave that is *in the mountain of God*.
It's hard to think of a much safer place than that!

Let's look at Moses, Exodus 33:12–23; 34:1–7:

Moses has got a tough job.
He has been told by God to lead the Israelites – easier said than done!

The Israelites are, well, human.
They argue, disobey, think they know best . . .

In the end Moses says to God, 'OK, if I am going to lead
these people, I need to know that you are with me. I
need some back-up here.'
So God promises Moses that he will be there
every step of the way.

Then Moses decides to ask for something more.

He says to God, 'show me your glory'.
Show me your glory . . .
Have you ever asked God that?
Asked him to show you his glory?

Moses is having a pretty tough time at the moment; the
Israelites have blatantly rebelled and ignored him.
And what does he say to God?
Show me your glory. I need more of you.
If I am going to do this, if I am going to lead these
people, I need to know how big my God is.
And God says, 'OK.' In a way, anyway!

God will let all his goodness pass before Moses.
He will proclaim his name to Moses.
But he will not allow Moses to see his face.

Why?

To protect Moses.
If Moses sees God's face, he will die.
No one can see God's face and live.
And God wants Moses alive!

So God hides Moses in a cleft in the rock and covers
Moses with his hand until he has passed by. Then, once
he has passed, he allows Moses to look and see his back.
Not his face, because God wants Moses alive.

When God says 'no' to us, could it be to make us more
spiritually alive?
To refine us?
To make us more like Jesus?

We know he loves us and wants the best for us – look at
the 'yesses' we already have!
His presence, guidance, love, protection, comfort, and
so much, much more.
Yes, yes, yes, yes, yes!

So, could it be that when he says no, it is for our own good?

Look what happens after God says 'no' to Moses:
Moses is given the Ten Commandments, is the only one
allowed up the mountain into God's presence and is
given (more) assurance from God that he will go with
Moses and the people.
Pretty good things, things that would draw Moses closer
to God.

And all things that Moses would have missed if God had said 'yes'.
If God had shown Moses his face and so allowed Moses to die.

It seems that God had good reason for saying 'no'!
He knew the bigger picture, just like he does today.

God says:
'I know the plans I have for you . . . plans to prosper you and not to harm you, plans to give you hope and a future' (Jeremiah 29:11).

Lord God,

'No' can be a hard word to hear.
Help me to remember that you only ever say it with my best interests at heart.
Thank you that you are in control.

Amen

Be an Elijah

Accept God's
'no'

My response:

Day 26

Well, I spent the night in the cave, a welcome rest after all the travelling I had to do to get here! It's good to be able to stop.

Finally Elijah seems to be giving himself a bit of a break. After being on the run from Jezebel, then being suicidal, then travelling without rest for forty days and nights, he stops. In a cave in the mountain of God.

Yesterday, we saw Moses hidden by God in a cleft in the rock.
Now we see Elijah safe in a cave/rock on the mountain of God.
Elijah stopped . . . physically and spiritually.

Physically he had covered a lot of ground recently, over two hundred miles from the desert to the mountain, and he also seems to have been all over the place spiritually.

A spiritual high on Carmel, a low when on the run from Jezebel, a low when giving up on life, a high when trying to reach the mountain of God . . . he probably needed to stop before he snapped!

Remember when God gave the Israelites the Ten Commandments? Exodus 20:8: 'Remember the Sabbath day by keeping it holy.'
And how were the people to do that?
By not working on that day.
By stopping the 'treadmill of life' – work, jobs etc. – on a regular basis.

Maybe God made it a commandment because he knew that the people would not be very good at stopping!

And not much has changed, has it?
Today, with all the technology we have, all the 24/7 communication, there is very little (if any) 'switch off' time.
Very little 'stop' time.

Ask yourself, when was the last time you stopped?
The last time you took a break?

Let's rewind right back to the beginning of Genesis, when God created the world. What do we see?
On day seven, *God rested*.
God set us an example and, if it is good enough for him, important enough for him to set the precedent, surely it is imperative for us.
God knew what he was doing when he gave us the fourth commandment!

But we need to do more than just stop.
We need to do more than just be still.

We need to take God's advice when he said
(Psalm 46:10, my italics):
'Be still *and know that I am God*.'

When was the last time you spent time just knowing
that God is God?
Recognizing that God is God?
Acknowledging that God is God?
Praising him?
Enjoying him?
Thinking about him . . . while deliberately NOT thinking
about all that you have going on in your life?

Seven is a pretty small number.
God only had seven days to fit everything into, but he
thought that resting, stopping, taking time out to enjoy
things was so important that he allocated a whole day
for it – and who are we to disregard the creator of the
universe?

Lord God,

It's hard to stop.
I am scared of what will happen if I do.
But I know I need to rest, so please help me.
And help me to enjoy it when I do!
To enjoy it with you.

Amen

Be an Elijah

Rest!

My response:

Day 27

God spoke to me in the cave. Actually, he asked me a question – what was I doing there? At first I thought I had misunderstood. Wasn't it obvious?! I have been doing my best for God, but people are trying to kill me anyway . . . I've been on the run . . . and now I've stopped running, I have stopped at the mountain of God. Loads of the other prophets have been killed. In fact, I'm the only one left! To be honest, I'm not sure what is going on. And then God told me to go out of the cave and stand on the mountain. Because his presence was about to pass by. So I went out and I did not have to wait long – a really strong wind came, rocks were flying everywhere! I just knew this must be God . . . but it wasn't. He wasn't there. Then an earthquake came. This must be it, I thought . . . but it wasn't. Nor was God in the fire that came afterwards. I was really disappointed. I'd obviously misunderstood what God had said.

And I could really do with some assurance that God is with me right now, as well!

I was about to turn back to the cave. And that's when I heard it. A gentle whisper. And God was there.

So, every week, God gives us a Sunday.
A day to rest.
A day to recharge.
A day to relax and enjoy worshipping him.

But then Monday comes.
And we have to head back out into the world.
To our jobs.
To our meetings.
To our day-to-day routine.

Elijah could not stay in that cave forever, however much he may have wanted to.
Just as we can't stay in Sunday forever . . . Monday comes.

So God tells Elijah to go out of the cave but, crucially, God's presence is still there.
He is not only with Elijah in the cave, he is there when Elijah goes out, too.
Just as when he tells you to head into your week, his presence goes with you.

Let's take a look at *how* God showed himself to Elijah.
Not in the wind, or earthquake, or fire.
Not in the big, impressive things that God might be expected to use to show himself.
No, it was in a gentle whisper.
But let's not forget, God still sent the wind, and the earthquake, and the fire.
He sent them.

And he could have revealed himself through them.
He just chose not to.
Sometimes, through expecting God to be in the 'wind,
earthquake, fire', we risk missing him.
Missing what he is doing.
Missing how he chooses to reveal himself.
Missing his gentle whisper.

Let's look at Naaman, 2 Kings 5:

Naaman was an important man.
He was a commander of the king of Aram's army.
Aram was a strong nation which had taken some of the
Israelites as prisoners.
Including a girl who became Naaman's slave.

Naaman was powerful, respected, a good soldier . . . but
he had leprosy.
His slave girl mentioned a prophet to him, Elisha, who
she knew could cure Naaman.
And so Naaman went to see Elisha.
He went in his chariot and stopped right outside Elisha's
house, expecting Elisha to come out and see him.

But Elisha just sent him a message.
And that message told Naaman to go and wash in the
River Jordan seven times.
If he did so, the leprosy would go.
Naaman would be healed.

Rather than being pleased that his leprosy days were over, Naaman was angry.
In fact he was fuming.
He had been expecting Elisha to come to him and perform some sort of dramatic, showy healing.
And so Naaman missed out on being healed.

Missed out on what God was doing.
All because Naaman expected something big.
Thought he deserved something big.

Thankfully, Naaman did see sense in the end.
He dipped himself in the river.
And he was healed.

Naaman learned that God is a God who reveals himself in small things.

Elijah learned that God is a God who reveals himself in small things.

In a whisper that was for Elijah's ears only.
A whisper that said, 'I'm here.'

Just as God whispers to you, every day, for your ears only, 'I'm here.'

'I'm here.'

Day 27

Lord God,

Your whisper is so precious to me.
Help me not to let it get drowned out in the noise
of life.
Thank you that you are here.

Amen

Be an Elijah

Listen for God's whisper

My response:

Day 28

When I heard the whisper, I knew it was God. So I went and stood at the entrance to the cave.
I was so aware of God's presence – the whisper was more powerful than an earthquake, that's for sure! But then God asked me again what I was doing there. Why would he ask me again?! Anyway, I explained again, exactly as I had before.

And this time God told me to go back the way I came.

Great. So I have to go back. Back to all the things I have been running from? Back past the places where I had really difficult times? Back to who knows what kind of reception? Back to being the only one?

Everyone hates me. But, as always, God must have known what I was thinking – and apparently there are actually 7,000 people in Israel who refuse to worship Baal. So much for me being the only one! Right, time to get going . . .

Let's look at the parable of the lost son
(Luke 15:11–32):

A man has left home.
Left his father.
Left his family.

And now he is alone.
No food.
No money.
He is sitting in a field.
With pigs.

He looks around at that muddy field.
And he thinks, 'What am I doing here?'

Just as God said to Elijah, 'What are you doing here?'

How would you answer?
Have you asked yourself, 'What am I doing here?'
It's a good question to ask, and not just once.
Ask it continually as you go through life:
What am I doing here?
Am I where God wants me to be?
Physically, emotionally, spiritually?
Am I making a difference for God?
Am I pleasing him? What am I doing here?

So the man realizes that he is in the wrong place and
decides to go back home.
Even though going back means a long journey, reliving
painful memories on the way, unsure whether he will be
welcome when he gets there, he decides to go home.

Just like Elijah.
God tells Elijah to go back despite the tough times he
will inevitably re-live on the way.

Could it be that God wants Elijah to face things?
To not pretend they didn't happen?
To deal with them . . . and then move on?

Sometimes we need to do that.
We need to acknowledge our fears and failures before
God . . . and then move on.

Psalm 103:12:
'as far as the east is from the west, so far has [God]
removed our transgressions from us.'
They've gone – move on!

So, the man plods on until he reaches home.
Nervous, unsure, fearing rejection, expecting that no
one will want to see him, he continues homeward.
And when he eventually gets there, he is welcomed.
By lots of people.
And he realizes that he is not alone.

Just like Elijah discovering that rather than being alone,
there are actually 7,000 people on his side. He had been
worrying unnecessarily all this time!

Don't worry unnecessarily – God has things sorted.
As the saying goes, 'Do not worry about tomorrow –
God is already there.'

Remember – you have a God who is in your tomorrows.
All of them.

Lord God,

What am I doing here?
I only want to be here if here is where you want me to be.
Please help me to always follow you,
so that I am never where you don't want me to be.
Thank you that you are in my tomorrows.

Amen

Be an Elijah

What am I
doing here?

My response:

Day 29

The journey back wasn't nearly as bad as I'd thought it would be. It was good to pass the place where I wanted to die. To move past it and move on. I feel like a different person now than I was then. It was so good to spend that time with God on the mountain.

And God told me to go and find someone called Elisha, who is going to be my assistant. God is so good. He knows I am getting on a bit and can't do what I used to, so he sorts it out.

I found Elisha ploughing a field, driving the oxen. When I told him that God wanted him to work with me, he went and said goodbye to his parents. Then he killed his oxen. He burned his ploughing equipment to make a fire to cook the oxen and gave the meat to the people around. And then he, Elisha, came with me. He travels with me everywhere I go now, watching and learning.

Elijah is back, in more ways than one.
He's moved on from the past, so is ready to face the future.
And the future involves Elisha.
Remember the angel telling Elijah that the journey was too much for him?

Well, he's not going to have to do it on his own any
more.

Let's take a look at Adam and Eve:
Adam is in the Garden of Eden, surrounded by beauty,
birds, animals . . . and yet what does God say?
'It is not good for the man to be alone.' (Genesis 2:18)
So he creates a companion for Adam.

And then Adam was no longer alone – he had Eve.
Just as Elijah was no longer alone – he had Elisha.

Ecclesiastes 4:9,10:
'Two are better than one . . . If one falls down, his friend
can help him up.'

And you are not alone.
At least, you don't need to be.
You have a family in God.
Make sure you meet with other Christians – don't ignore
your family!

'Let us not give up meeting together . . . but let us
encourage one another'
(Hebrews 10:25).

And, as Elijah discovered, meeting together and
knowing there are other Christians out there is an
encouragement in itself.

But what about Elisha, who has suddenly appeared on the scene?

One day, Elisha is just getting on with his day job.
Ploughing a field, minding his own business, when along comes Elijah.
With a message from God.
A message that will turn Elisha's life upside down.

Messages from God can do that!
God is in the business of changing lives . . . are you letting him change yours?

When Elijah sees Elisha, he throws his cloak on Elisha.
Probably not because Elisha was cold – ploughing with oxen is pretty hard work!
No, there was a deeper significance . . .

In those days, a person's cloak was the most important type of clothing that they could own. Apart from offering warmth, comfort and protection, it could be used as an 'I owe you' for a debt. It could be torn into pieces to show grief. And it could be used as Elijah used it, to show who would be one's successor.
And the person who would be taking over from Elijah was Elisha.

Elisha had some pretty big shoes to fill.
But he was willing to step into them, because God wanted him to.

Day 29

Are you willing to do what God wants you to do, however daunting it may seem?

God was moving Elisha in a new direction and, for Elisha, that meant completely getting rid of his old life – he said goodbye to his parents, he slaughtered his oxen and he burned his tools.
His parents were probably not bad people! Elisha must have had a good relationship with them if he wanted to go and see them before following Elijah. They were his first thought. But, clinging on to them would have hindered Elisha's new calling.
His parents were not going anywhere so, unless he left them, Elisha was not going anywhere either.

Do friends/other people sometimes stop you from moving on, from moving with God?
Unintentionally or deliberately, do they get in the way of your relationship with him?
Where possible, maybe you need to follow Elisha's example and say 'goodbye'.

And not just goodbye to unhelpful friendships.
What about material things?

It can be hard to say goodbye to material things, can't it?
You know they are still there, lurking in the cupboard.
Or in the shop.
Easily accessible.

What did Elisha do with material things? With his work tools?
He destroyed them! He did not need them any more.
They were symbolic of his old life.
God was changing his direction . . . and Elisha was not going back.

Sometimes, goodbye is not enough – we need to get rid.

'Put off your old self . . . and . . . put on the new self, created to be like God in true righteousness and holiness' (Ephesians 4:22–24).

Put off and put on.

Elisha did not just get rid of his old life.
Did not just leave a gap.
He filled the gap.
Filled it with the new life God had for him.
And that is crucial.
When things are taken away from us – by ourselves, by other people, by God – it is so important to fill the gaps.
And to be sure to fill them with God.

Next time you feel empty, feel that things are hard, feel that things have been taken away, feel that you have nothing left but gaps . . . let God come in.
Let his presence fill your empty spaces.
Let him fill the gaps.

Day 29

Lord God,

Sometimes it is hard when life changes.
Goodbyes can be tough.
When I have to say 'goodbye', help me to follow it
with 'hello' to whatever you have in store for me.
Help me to fill the gaps with you.

Amen

Be an Elijah

Fill the gaps
with God

My response:

Day 30

It's Elisha here. I have just found Elijah's diary and I want to finish it for him. It just needs one more entry. As Elijah said, I went everywhere with him. But then, one day, he told me that he was going to Bethel, but that I should stay behind. I refused and went with him anyway! When we got there, some prophets asked me if I knew that God would take Elijah away from me that day. As it turned out, I did know and I told them not to talk about it – who wants to be reminded that their fantastic mentor is leaving this earth? The same thing happened again in Jericho. And at the River Jordan. Elijah had not wanted me to go with him, but I had gone anyway.

When we got to the Jordan, Elijah hit the water with his cloak. The water divided and the two of us walked over on dry ground.

Then Elijah got straight to the point. He knew that God was going to take him and so he asked me what he could do for me before that happened. I looked at him. This amazing man of God. My mentor, my friend, my example, the man I want to be . . . and I could only think of one thing to ask for. Could I really be the one that would carry on his work? Could I inherit his spirit, his work, his calling? Maybe that was unfair; I know it was not up to Elijah. But Elijah answered me by saying that if I saw him when God took him, the answer to my request would be yes. And guess what? I did see him! Horses and a chariot of fire came and whisked Elijah up to heaven. So the answer was yes! I picked up Elijah's cloak and looked at the River Jordan. Was Elijah's God still here? I struck the river. And the water parted, just as it had for Elijah. I crossed over, with the Spirit of Elijah resting on me. Crossed over to carry on the work Elijah started. Crossed over to carry on the journey with Elijah's God. His God and mine.

So, Elijah is gone.
Now, imagine Elisha standing there, looking into the sky.
Eventually, he looks down and sees Elijah's cloak.
He picks it up.
And the transfer is complete.
Elijah initiated this when he called Elisha to follow him and now, having followed him, Elisha is being sent out to take over.
Elijah's cloak is now Elisha's.
Elijah's journey is now Elisha's, with the spirit and essence of Elijah going with him.

After Jesus died and rose again, he appeared to his disciples and then breathed his spirit on them
(see John 20:22).
Jesus' work on earth was nearly over.
In a sense, Jesus passed the baton on.

He gave the disciples his cloak.
His journey, his physical presence on earth, was now theirs.

Matthew 28:19,20 tells us that before he was taken to heaven, Jesus' instructions to his disciples were to 'go and make disciples of all nations'.
They were to go and tell people the good news about Jesus.
But, Jesus added, you won't be alone – 'I am with you always'.

Jesus' presence went with the disciples, just as Elijah's cloak went with Elisha.

When the disciples died, Jesus' presence would be with other people.
Because the disciples had passed on the good news.
And then the other people would pass it on . . . and so on . . . and so on . . . and so on . . . until it reached you.

Will you pass it on?
Pass on the good news about Jesus?
Or will the chain stop with you?

Elijah left a wonderful legacy for Elisha.
A legacy of how to be a man of God.

Jesus left a wonderful legacy for his disciples.

A legacy of his presence and how to share it.
What will your spiritual legacy be?
What will you leave behind?
People who have grown closer to God because of you?

And so, as Elijah's journey ends, Elisha's begins – fuelled by the legacy that Elijah left him.
A legacy of a godly life.

Lord God,

Thank you for all the people who have passed your good news on until it reached me.
Wow!
Help the chain not to stop with me;
help me to leave a legacy for you.

Amen

Be an Elijah

Leave a
legacy

My response:

You can read more about Emily and her books at:

facebook.com/profile.
php?id=100005373166724&fref=ts
or
twitter.com/EmilyOwenAuthor

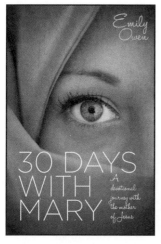

30 Days with Mary
A devotional journey with the mother of Jesus
Emily Owen

What must it have been like to be Mary, the mother of the Son of God?

In *30 Days with Mary* we look at her diary, sharing in her trials and challenges, fears and joys, from her teenage encounter with an angel, to the awesomeness of realizing her crucified son is alive again. The diary excerpts lead us in contemplation, challenging our own relationship with Christ and, in so doing, draw us closer to him.

978-1-86024-935-8

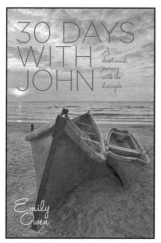

30 Days with John
A devotional journey with the disciple
Emily Owen

If John, the disciple of Jesus, had written a diary, what would it be like? Here is a chance to find out, from the baptism of Jesus, through his ministry, to his death and the astounding news that Jesus is alive, and then afterwards as John grows older . . .

The thirty days of 'diary extracts', followed by thought-provoking teaching and questions, provide an interesting, contemplative yet gently challenging read.

978-1-86024-936-5